This Is My Dentist

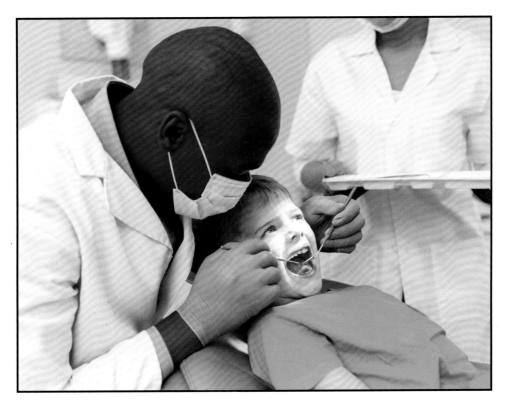

Adam Bellamy

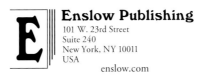

Enslow Publishing
101 W. 23rd Street
Suite 240
New York, NY 10011
USA

enslow.com

Published in 2017 by Enslow Publishing, LLC.
101 W. 23rd Street, Suite 240, New York, NY 10011

Library of Congress Cataloguing-in-Publication Data
Names: Bellamy, Adam, author.
Title: This is my dentist / Adam Bellamy.
Description: New York, NY : Enslow Publishing, LLC, [2017] | Series: All about my world | Audience: Ages 5 up. | Audience: Pre-school, excluding K.| Includes bibliographical references and index.
Identifiers: LCCN 2016022715| ISBN 9780766080966 (library bound) | ISBN 9780766080942 (pbk.) | ISBN 9780766080959 (6-pack)
Subjects: LCSH: Dentistry—Juvenile literature.
Classification: LCC RK63 .B45 2017 | DDC 617.6—dc23
LC record available at https://lccn.loc.gov/2016022715

Printed in China

Photo Credits: Cover, pp. 1, 12 michaeljung/Shutterstock.com; peiyang/Shutterstock.com (globe icon on spine); pp. 3 (left), 6 RomanSo/Shutterstock.com; pp. 3 (center), 8 © iStockphoto.com/DragonImages; pp. 3 (right), 10 S. Castelli/Shutterstock.com; pp. 4–5 Donskaya Olga/Shutterstock.com; p. 14 Rob van Esch/Shutterstock.com; p. 16 TinnaPong/Shutterstock.com; p. 18 © iStockphoto.com/fotografstockholm; p. 20 © iStockphoto.com/XiXinXing; p. 22 Tatyana Vyc/Shutterstock.com.

Contents

Words to Know

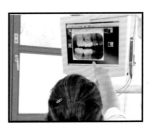

dentist   hygienist   X-ray

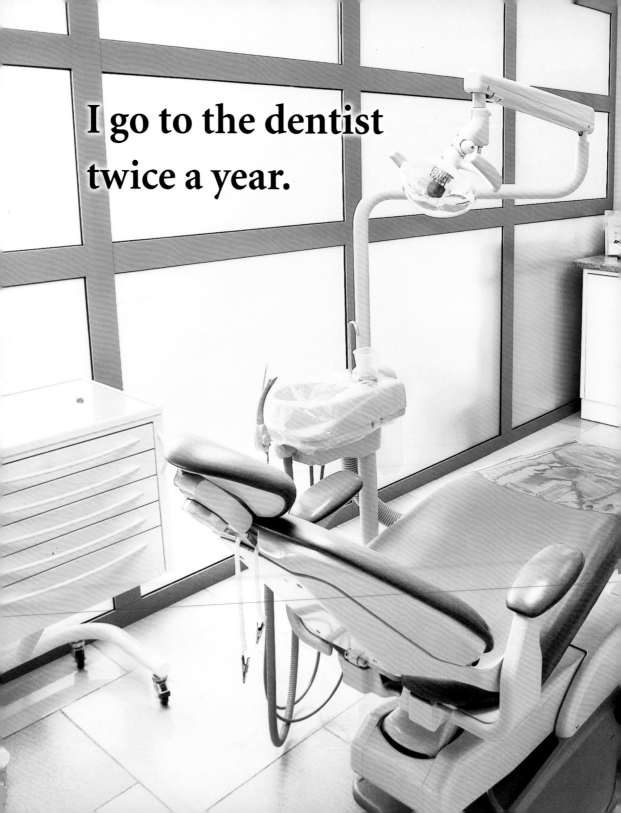

I go to the dentist
twice a year.

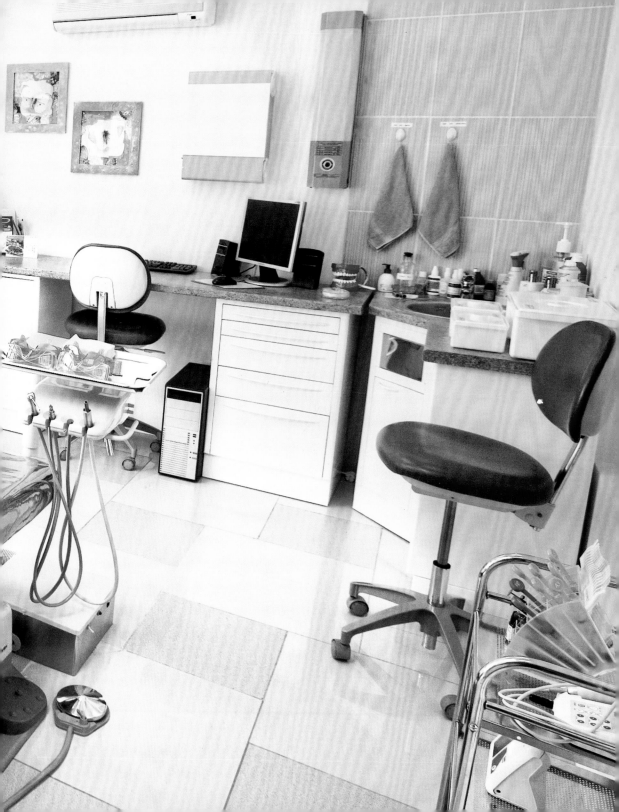

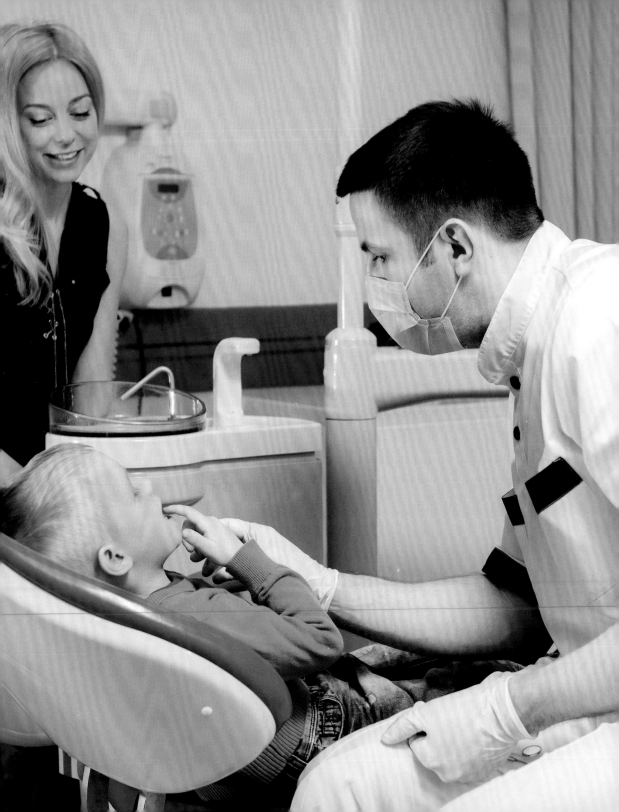

The dentist is a doctor for teeth.

I sit in the chair. The hygienist cleans my teeth.

She also takes X-rays of my teeth. She makes sure my teeth are growing correctly.

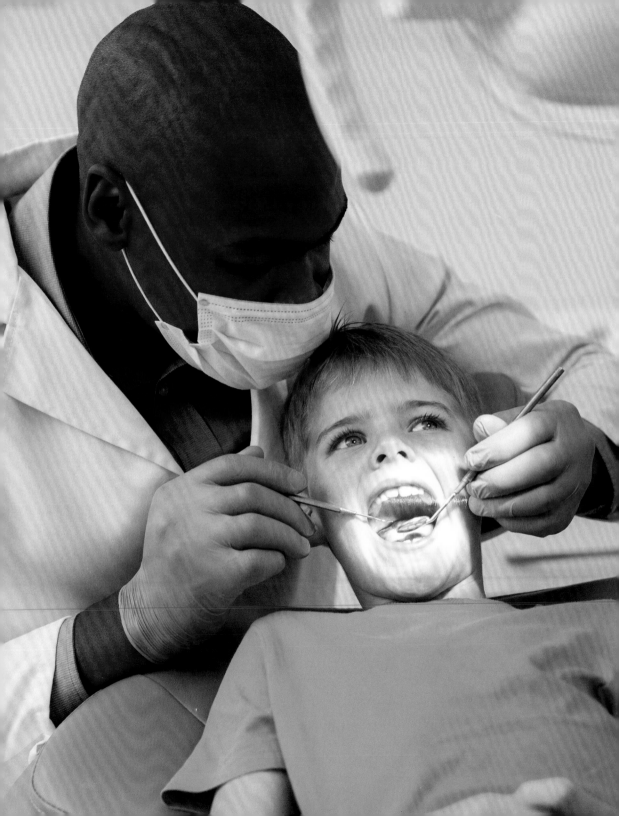

Then the dentist looks at my teeth. He says my baby teeth are loose.

When my baby teeth fall out, my adult teeth come in!

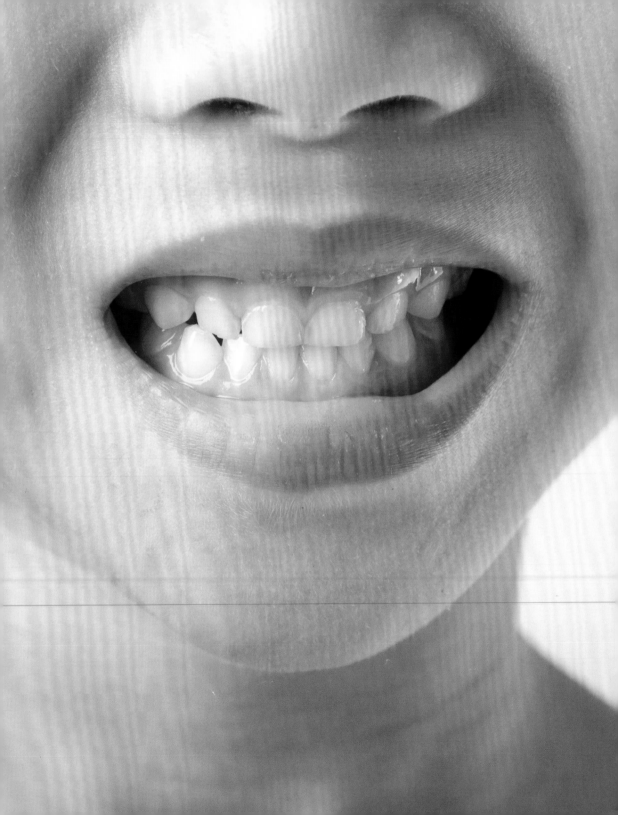

The dentist says my teeth are healthy. I have no cavities! Cavities are bad for your teeth.

I always get a new toothbrush, floss, and toothpaste.

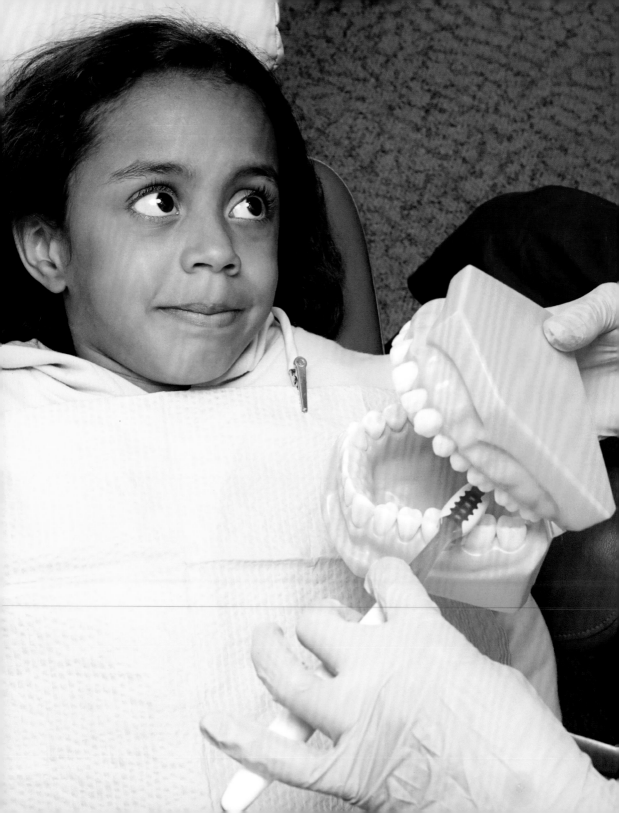

It is important for me to take good care of my teeth. The dentist helps me do that.

My teeth feel clean after I visit the dentist!

Read More

Finnigan, Sean. *Going to the Dentist*. Northampton, MA: Pioneer Valley Books, 2012.

Hewitt, Sally. *Going to the Dentist* (Looking After Me). Minneapolis, MN: QED Publishing, 2015.

Mcguire, Leslie, and Jean Pidgeon. *Brush Your Teeth Please: A Pop-Up Book*. New York, NY: Reader's Digest, 2013.

Websites

Cavity Free Kids
cavityfreekids.org
Activities, games, and information about keeping teeth healthy!

KidsHealth
kidshealth.org/en/kids/go-dentist.html
Learn about going to the dentist and how to take care of your teeth.

Mouth Healthy Kids
www.mouthhealthykids.org/en/
Watch videos, play games, and take fun quizzes.

Index

Guided Reading Level: E
Guided Reading Leveling System is based on the guidelines recommended by Fountas and Pinnell.

Word Count: 118